MW00957150

Exploring Maui

Your Ultimate Pocket Size Maui Travel Guide 2023-2024 Book For A Perfect Hawaiian Vacation

Willie F. Smith

Copyright 2023 © Willie F. Smith All rights reserved.

No part of this book may be reproduced in any form or by any electronic or mechanical means, including information storage and retrieval systems, without permission in writing from the publisher, except by a reviewer who may quote brief passages in a review. This book is a work of non-fiction. The views and opinions expressed in this book are the author'sb own and do not necessarily reflect those of the publisher or any other person or organization. The information in this book is provided for educational and informational purposes only. It is not intended as a substitute for professional advice of any kind.

Table Of Content

Introduction

In the heart of the Pacific Ocean, lies the paradise known as Maui, an island that sings with the melodies of turquoise waves and whispers the tales of ancient volcanoes. As I stepped onto its shores, a sense of anticipation coursed through my veins, for I was about to embark on a wondrous exploration of this tropical haven.

My first encounter with Maui's breathtaking beauty took place along the legendary Road to Hana. Winding through lush rainforests and cascading waterfalls, each bend in the road unveiled a new natural wonder. The air was thick with the fragrance of tropical flowers, and the melodies of chirping birds echoed in harmony with the rush of nearby streams. As I stood beneath the majestic Wailua Falls, its cascading waters painting the landscape in shimmering hues, I felt a profound connection with the raw power and untouched beauty of nature.

Eager to delve deeper into the island's mystique, I embarked on an adventure to Haleakala National Park, home to the dormant volcano that shares its name. Before dawn broke, I ascended to the summit, shrouded in a blanket of darkness. As the first rays of sunlight pierced through the horizon, an otherworldly scene unfolded before my eyes. The sky erupted in a vibrant palette of purples, pinks, and oranges, while the vast crater, blanketed in an ethereal mist, seemed like a portal to another realm. Witnessing the birth of a new day atop Haleakala was an experience that left me in awe of the Earth's immense power and eternal beauty.

Maui's allure extended beyond its natural wonders; its warm embrace of culture and tradition beckoned me to explore further. I found myself captivated by the spirit of aloha as I delved into the island's rich heritage. I immersed myself in the rhythmic chants and graceful hula dances, learning the stories and legends that have shaped the island's identity for generations. The warmth and hospitality of the locals were infectious, and I felt embraced as a member of the island's ohana (family).

No exploration of Maui would be complete without basking in its crystal-clear waters. I embarked on a snorkeling adventure off the coast of Molokini, a crescent-shaped volcanic crater teeming with vibrant marine life. Descending into the turquoise depths, I entered an underwater wonderland. Schools of tropical fish danced amidst coral gardens, and graceful sea turtles glided through the cerulean waters. With each stroke of my fins, I felt a deep sense of gratitude for the fragile ecosystem that thrives beneath the waves.

As the sun began its descent, I found solace in the tranquility of Kaanapali Beach. With its powdery white sands and swaying palm trees, it was a picture-perfect paradise. As the fiery sun dipped into the horizon, casting its golden glow across the sky, I reflected on the magic of Maui—the island that had stolen my heart. In that moment, I realized that Maui was not just a destination; it was a state of mind, a feeling of serenity and wonder that stayed with me long after I left its shores.

As I bid farewell to Maui, I carried its mystical charm within me, a treasure of memories etched into my soul. The island had taught me to appreciate the raw beauty of nature, to embrace different cultures, and to find joy in the simplest moments. Maui had awakened my spirit of adventure and reconnected me with the essence of life itself. And as I journeyed back to the mainland, I knew that Maui would forever hold a special place in my heart—a timeless reminder of the wonders that await those who dare to explore.

CHAPTER 1

Welcome to Maui

Welcome to "Exploring Maui: A Comprehensive Travel Guide." In this guide, we invite you to embark on an extraordinary journey to the enchanting Hawaiian island of Maui. Known as the Valley Isle, Maui is renowned for its breathtaking natural beauty, vibrant culture, and warm hospitality. Whether you are a first-time visitor or a seasoned traveler returning to this paradise, Maui offers a wealth of experiences that will captivate your senses and leave you with lifelong memories.

A Brief Introduction to the Island

Stretching across 727 square miles, Maui is the second-largest island in the Hawaiian archipelago. It is located in the central Pacific Ocean and is part of the state of Hawaii, which consists of a chain of volcanic islands formed millions of years ago. Maui's volcanic origins have bestowed upon it a diverse and captivating landscape that attracts visitors from around the world.

History and Cultural Significance

Maui has a rich history dating back centuries, shaped by the ancient Polynesians who settled here. Their fascinating traditions, legends, and customs have been passed down through generations, contributing to the island's unique cultural tapestry. The historical significance of Maui can be witnessed in its ancient temples, known as heiaus, and sacred sites that pay homage to the island's spiritual heritage.

Geography and Climate Overview

Maui's geography is a true testament to nature's artistry. The island is characterized by dramatic contrasts, featuring towering volcanic peaks, lush rainforests, cascading waterfalls, pristine beaches, and vibrant coral reefs. The crown jewel of Maui is the majestic Haleakala, a dormant volcano soaring to an elevation of 10,023 feet above sea level. Its otherworldly landscape, often shrouded in mist and bathed in ethereal hues, provides a truly awe-inspiring experience.

Maui's climate is characterized by mild temperatures year-round, making it an ideal tropical getaway. The island enjoys abundant sunshine, with coastal areas offering a pleasant breeze. The eastern side of the island receives more rainfall, resulting in lush rainforests and vibrant vegetation. These favorable climatic conditions create a paradise for outdoor activities and allow for the growth of unique flora and fauna.

The Spirit of Aloha

Maui is synonymous with the spirit of aloha—a concept deeply ingrained in the Hawaiian culture. Aloha extends beyond a mere greeting; it embodies a way of life rooted in kindness, harmony, and respect for others and the natural world. Maui's residents, known as kama'aina, embody this spirit and welcome visitors with open arms, sharing their love for the island and its traditions.

The spirit of aloha can be felt in every aspect of Maui, from the warm smiles of locals to the rhythmic chants and melodic tunes of Hawaiian music. It permeates the island's vibrant festivals, such as the renowned Maui County Fair and the lively celebration of Aloha Festivals. Visitors are encouraged to embrace the spirit of aloha, to immerse themselves in the island's culture, and to approach their journey with an open heart and a sense of reverence.

CHAPTER 2

Planning Your Trip

Climate and Best Times to Visit

Maui enjoys a mild and pleasant climate throughout the year, making it a popular destination for travelers. However, it's essential to be aware of weather patterns and plan your visit accordingly.

Maui experiences two main seasons: the dry season (April to October) and the wet season (November to March). The dry season typically offers sunny days with warm temperatures, while the wet season brings occasional rainfall, particularly in the form of afternoon showers. Be prepared for sudden weather changes and pack accordingly.

The best time to visit Maui depends on your preferences and activities. The shoulder seasons of spring (April to May) and fall (September to November) often offer pleasant weather, fewer crowds, and better prices. However, the summer months (June to August) are popular for family vacations, and winter (December to February) attracts surfers seeking larger waves.

What to Pack

When packing for your Maui adventure, it's important to consider the island's tropical climate and various activities you'll engage in. Here are some essential items to include in your suitcase:

1. Lightweight clothing: Pack breathable and comfortable clothing suitable for warm weather, such as shorts, t-shirts, sundresses, and swimwear.

2. Sun protection: Don't forget to bring sunscreen with a high SPF, a wide-brimmed hat, sunglasses, and a beach umbrella to shield yourself from the sun's rays.

3. Footwear: Include comfortable walking shoes for exploring, flip-flops or sandals for the beach, and water shoes for activities like snorkeling or hiking.

4. Outdoor gear: If you plan on engaging in outdoor activities, consider packing a lightweight rain jacket, hiking boots, snorkeling gear, and a reusable water bottle.

5. Electronics and accessories: Remember to bring your camera, charger, power adapters, and any other electronics you may need. A waterproof phone case or pouch is also handy for water-related adventures.

Entry Requirements and Visa

Before traveling to Maui, it's important to ensure you have the necessary entry requirements and valid travel documents. Here are some key points to keep in mind:

1. Passport: Ensure your passport is valid for at least six months beyond your intended stay in Maui.

2. Visa: Depending on your nationality, you may be eligible for the Visa Waiver Program, which allows for visa-free entry for up to 90 days. However, it's crucial to check the specific visa requirements for your country of citizenship before traveling.

Getting to Maui

Maui is well-connected to major airports in the United States and international destinations. Here are some common ways to reach the island:

1. Air travel: The most convenient way to reach Maui is by flying into Kahului Airport (OGG), which serves both domestic and international flights. Several airlines offer direct flights to Maui from mainland U.S. cities, as well as international destinations like Canada and Japan.

2. Inter-island flights: If you're already in Hawaii or planning to visit other islands, consider taking an inter-island flight from Honolulu International Airport (HNL) or other Hawaiian airports to reach Maui.

Getting Around

Once you've arrived in Maui, you'll need to determine the best transportation options to explore the island. Here are some methods for getting around:

1. Rental car: Renting a car provides the most flexibility for exploring Maui, as it allows you to navigate the island at your own pace. Several car rental companies operate at the airports and major towns on the island.

2. Public transportation: The Maui Bus offers an affordable option for traveling between major towns

and popular attractions. However, keep in mind that the bus service may have limited routes and schedules, so plan accordingly.

3. Taxis and ridesharing: Taxis are available in Maui, primarily at the airports and larger towns. Ridesharing services like Uber and Lyft are also available on the island.

Currency and Money Matters

The official currency of Maui is the U.S. dollar. Here are some important considerations regarding currency and money matters:

1. Currency exchange: It's advisable to exchange currency before arriving in Maui, as exchange services on the island may have limited availability and higher fees.

2. ATMs and credit cards: ATMs are widely available in Maui, and credit cards are accepted at most establishments. However, it's recommended to carry some cash for smaller vendors and rural areas where card acceptance may be limited.

CHAPTER 3

Getting to Know Maui

Maui's Regions

Lahaina and Kaanapali

Located on the western coast of Maui, Lahaina and Kaanapali are popular destinations known for their stunning beaches, vibrant nightlife, and rich history. Lahaina, once a bustling whaling village, has preserved its historic charm with beautifully restored buildings that now house art galleries, boutique shops, and exquisite restaurants. Stroll along Front Street, Lahaina's main thoroughfare, and immerse yourself in its vibrant atmosphere.

Just north of Lahaina lies the resort area of Kaanapali. Boasting pristine white sand beaches, luxury resorts, and world-class golf courses, Kaanapali offers a perfect blend of relaxation and recreation. Take a leisurely walk along the Kaanapali Beachwalk, indulge in watersports, or witness the breathtaking sunset from the iconic Black Rock (Pu'u Keka'a).

Kihei and Wailea

Located on the sunny southwestern coast, Kihei and Wailea are popular beachfront communities renowned for their beautiful beaches, resort amenities, and stunning ocean views. Kihei offers a laid-back atmosphere with a range of accommodations, from affordable condos to beachfront resorts. Its long stretches of sandy beaches, such as Kamaole Beach Park, are ideal for swimming, sunbathing, and snorkeling.

Just south of Kihei, the upscale resort area of Wailea awaits. Known for its luxury hotels, world-class golf courses, and exquisite dining, Wailea offers a refined and indulgent experience. Explore the picturesque Wailea Coastal Path, pamper yourself at one of the renowned spas, or tee off at championship golf courses with breathtaking ocean views.

Paia and Hana

Located on the eastern coast of Maui, Paia and Hana offer a glimpse into the island's more laid-back and bohemian side. Paia, a charming town known as the gateway to the famous Road to Hana, exudes a vibrant and artistic atmosphere. Its eclectic shops, local boutiques, and organic eateries attract surfers, artists, and travelers seeking an alternative Maui experience.

Further along the Road to Hana lies the remote town of Hana. This secluded paradise is famous for its lush rainforests, cascading waterfalls, and black sand beaches. Immerse yourself in nature as you explore Wai'anapanapa State Park with its striking volcanic coastline or take a dip in the refreshing pools of Ohe'o Gulch, also known as the Seven Sacred Pools.

Upcountry Maui

Escape the coastal areas and venture into the picturesque Upcountry Maui. Located on the slopes of Haleakala volcano, this region offers cooler temperatures, rolling green hills, and panoramic views of the island. Experience the charm of towns like Makawao, known for its cowboy heritage and arts scene, or visit the Ali'i Kula Lavender Farm, where fragrant lavender fields create a serene and enchanting ambiance.

Explore the fertile landscapes of Kula and visit the Upcountry Maui's farms, wineries, and botanical gardens. Sample fresh produce at the Maui Tropical Plantation or embark on a scenic drive along the winding roads of the Kula Highway, offering breathtaking vistas of the island's central valley.

Molokai and Lanai

While not part of Maui itself, the neighboring islands of Molokai and Lanai are easily accessible from Maui and offer unique experiences for adventurous travelers. Molokai is known for its unspoiled beauty, rich cultural traditions, and its deep connection to the land. Explore the majestic sea cliffs of Kalaupapa National Historical Park or immerse yourself in the aloha spirit of the local community.

Lanai, often referred to as the "Pineapple Island," presents an exclusive and luxurious getaway. Indulge in world-class golfing at the Manele Golf Course, relax at the luxurious resorts, or embark on an off-road adventure to discover Lanai's secluded beaches and other natural wonders.

Best Beaches

Kaanapali Beach

Kaanapali Beach, located on Maui's western coast, is a world-class beach renowned for its long stretches of golden sand and vibrant atmosphere. This iconic beach stretches for three miles, providing ample space for sunbathing, swimming, and water activities. The beach is lined with luxury resorts, restaurants, and shops, creating a lively and convenient beachfront experience.

Kaanapali Beach offers excellent swimming conditions with its calm waters and gradual slope. Snorkelers can explore the vibrant underwater world just offshore, where colorful fish and turtles are often spotted. For those seeking adventure, Kaanapali is a popular spot for parasailing, jet skiing, and paddleboarding. As the day comes to a close, be sure to witness the mesmerizing sunset that paints the sky in vibrant hues, creating a truly magical experience.

Wailea Beach

Located in the upscale resort area of Wailea, Wailea Beach is known for its pristine beauty and luxurious ambiance. This crescent-shaped beach offers soft sands, gentle waves, and panoramic views of the Pacific Ocean. The beach is flanked by world-class resorts, providing easy access to amenities, beachfront dining, and water activities.

Wailea Beach is ideal for swimming and sunbathing, with its clear turquoise waters inviting visitors to take a refreshing dip. Snorkelers can explore the vibrant coral reefs just offshore, home to an array of tropical fish and marine life. The beach is also a popular spot for stand-up paddleboarding, kayaking, and bodyboarding. Unwind on the beach, rent a cabana, and enjoy the serenity and luxury that Wailea Beach has to offer.

Napili Bay

Nestled on Maui's northwest coast, Napili Bay is a hidden gem that offers a more secluded and intimate beach experience. This crescent-shaped bay boasts soft white sands, calm turquoise waters, and a serene atmosphere. The bay is sheltered by rocky outcroppings, creating a tranquil environment perfect for relaxation and swimming.

Snorkeling enthusiasts will delight in exploring the coral reefs teeming with colorful fish, located just a short swim from the shore. Napili Bay is also known for its excellent boogie boarding conditions, with small waves that are perfect for riders of all skill levels. The beach is surrounded by low-rise condominiums and small hotels, maintaining a peaceful and laid-back vibe. Enjoy a picnic on the beach, soak up the sun, and relish in the natural beauty that Napili Bay offers.

Hookipa Beach

For those seeking a beach that offers both stunning scenery and thrilling water sports, Hookipa Beach on Maui's northern coast is the perfect destination. Known as the windsurfing capital of the world, Hookipa Beach attracts windsurfers and kiteboarders from around the globe, who come to ride the legendary waves and harness the strong trade winds.

Even if you're not an experienced windsurfer, Hookipa Beach is still a sight to behold. Watch as skilled athletes gracefully glide across the water, performing impressive tricks and jumps. The beach is also a popular spot for surfing, with waves suitable for both beginners and more advanced surfers. If you prefer to stay on land, enjoy a leisurely stroll along the shoreline or find a comfortable spot to watch the surfers and enjoy the panoramic views of the rugged coastline.

Big Beach (Makena Beach)

Located in Makena, on Maui's southern coast, Big Beach, also known as Makena Beach, is a magnificent stretch of golden sand that lives up to its name. With its wide expanse of sand, clear blue waters, and untouched beauty, Big Beach offers a quintessential tropical paradise experience.

Big Beach is renowned for its impressive shore break, attracting bodyboarders and experienced swimmers looking for a thrill. Caution should be exercised when entering the water, as the waves can be powerful. However, the beach also offers calmer sections perfect for sunbathing and relaxation.

Nearby, Little Beach, a clothing-optional beach, is a popular spot for those seeking a more alternative beach experience.

As you explore Big Beach, take in the picturesque views of the neighboring islands of Kahoolawe and Molokini, which create a stunning backdrop to this pristine coastal paradise.

Exploring Maui's Towns

Lahaina

Lahaina, located on Maui's western coast, is a historic town that once served as a bustling whaling port. Today, it retains its charming, old-world character with beautifully preserved buildings that harken back to its prosperous past. Front Street, Lahaina's main thoroughfare, is lined with art galleries, boutique shops, and a plethora of restaurants and cafes.

As you wander through Lahaina, you'll encounter numerous landmarks that bear witness to its storied history. Visit the iconic Banyan Tree Park, home to one of the largest banyan trees in the world, which provides shade and a gathering spot for locals and visitors alike. Step into the Lahaina Courthouse, now a museum, to learn about the town's whaling era and its significance in Hawaiian history.

Lahaina is also known for its vibrant nightlife, with a plethora of bars and live music venues that come alive after the sun sets. Enjoy a sunset cruise from Lahaina Harbor, where you can witness the breathtaking colors of the evening sky while sipping on a refreshing cocktail.

Paia

Located on Maui's north shore, the laid-back town of Paia exudes a bohemian atmosphere that attracts artists, surfers, and travelers seeking an alternative Maui experience. This former sugar plantation town has transformed into a haven for artisans, with its streets lined with unique boutiques, galleries, and surf shops.

Paia is also known for its fantastic dining scene, offering a diverse range of restaurants and cafes serving organic and farm-to-table cuisine. Indulge in mouthwatering dishes crafted with fresh local ingredients, such as acai bowls, vegan delights, and traditional Hawaiian plate lunches.

Paia's proximity to the world-renowned surfing spot of Ho'okipa Beach makes it a hub for water sports enthusiasts. Watch as skilled surfers ride the waves, windsurfers harness the strong trade winds, and kiteboarders perform thrilling aerial maneuvers. If you're feeling adventurous, you can rent gear and join in the excitement.

Makawao

Nestled in the upcountry region of Maui, Makawao exudes a charming, rustic appeal. This small town is known for its paniolo (Hawaiian cowboy) heritage, evident in its storefronts adorned with cowboy hats and boots. Makawao's main street, Baldwin Avenue, is lined with boutique shops, art galleries, and local eateries.

Explore the town's unique shops, where you can find handmade jewelry, local artwork, and one-of-a-kind souvenirs. Makawao is also home to the Hui No'eau Visual Arts Center, where you can immerse yourself in Maui's art scene through exhibitions and workshops.

Don't miss the opportunity to visit the historic Makawao Union Church, a beautiful architectural gem that has been serving the community since the late 19th century. Nearby, you can witness the stunning views of the island from the summit of Haleakala volcano at the Polipoli Spring State Recreation Area.

Hana

Located on Maui's eastern coast, the town of Hana offers a glimpse into old Hawaii and a peaceful retreat from the bustling tourist areas. Hana is renowned for its untouched beauty, with lush rainforests, cascading waterfalls, and scenic coastal views.

Take the legendary Road to Hana, a winding highway that stretches for approximately 52 miles, offering breathtaking views at every turn. Along the way, you'll encounter enchanting waterfalls, such as the iconic Wailua Falls, and serene pools where you can take a refreshing dip, such as the Seven Sacred Pools (Ohe'o Gulch) in the Kipahulu District of Haleakala National Park.

In Hana town itself, explore the rich cultural heritage by visiting the Hana Cultural Center and Museum, which showcases the traditions and history of the local community. Indulge in the flavors of authentic Hawaiian cuisine at local food stands and restaurants, where you can savor traditional dishes like poi, kalua pork, and fresh seafood.

Wailuku

Wailuku, Maui's county seat, is nestled at the foothills of the West Maui Mountains. This historic town offers a blend of old-world charm and modern conveniences, making it an ideal place to experience local culture and explore Maui's historical roots.

Stroll along Market Street, Wailuku's main thoroughfare, and discover its eclectic shops, art galleries, and cafes. The town is home to the Bailey House Museum, which showcases Hawaiian artifacts and provides insight into the island's history and cultural heritage.

Wailuku is also known for its lively events and festivals. Don't miss the monthly Wailuku First Friday town party, where the streets come alive with live music, local vendors, and food trucks. During the holiday season, Wailuku hosts the festive Wailuku Christmas Parade, a beloved community tradition.

As you explore Wailuku, take a moment to appreciate the panoramic views of the Iao Valley, home to the iconic Iao Needle. This towering rock formation is a significant landmark in Hawaiian history and offers a glimpse into the island's geological wonders.

CHAPTER 4

Maui's Natural Wonders

Haleakala National Park

Haleakala National Park is a crown jewel of Maui, encompassing the majestic Haleakala volcano and its surrounding landscapes. This natural wonder is known for its dramatic volcanic crater, stunning sunrises, and unique flora and fauna. The park is divided into two distinct districts: the Summit District and the Kipahulu District.

Summit District

The Summit District is located at the summit of Haleakala volcano, reaching an elevation of 10,023 feet above sea level. The landscape here resembles a lunar-like expanse, with rugged volcanic terrain and panoramic views that stretch across the island. One of the most popular activities in the Summit District is witnessing the sunrise from the summit. Visitors often wake up early to make the journey and experience the breathtaking moment when the sun emerges from the horizon, casting vibrant colors across the sky.

In addition to the sunrise, the Summit District offers incredible hiking opportunities. The Halemau'u Trail takes hikers through a stunning desert-like landscape, surrounded by cinder cones and endemic plant species. The Sliding Sands Trail, also known as Keonehe'ehe'e Trail, leads adventurers into the crater, allowing them to explore its otherworldly terrain. Along the trails, keep an eye out for unique plant life, including the silversword, a rare and protected species found only on Haleakala.

Kipahulu District

The Kipahulu District, located on Maui's eastern coast, offers a stark contrast to the summit. Here, lush rainforests, cascading waterfalls, and freshwater pools await. The main highlight of the Kipahulu District is the Pipiwai Trail, a 4-mile round-trip hike that takes visitors through a dense bamboo forest, past towering waterfalls, and to the majestic Waimoku Falls.

The Kipahulu District is also home to the Pools of 'Ohe'o, also known as the Seven Sacred Pools. These tiered pools, fed by freshwater streams, create a series of natural swimming holes that are perfect for a refreshing dip. Visitors can relax in the cool waters, surrounded by the lush tropical vegetation of the area.

Road to Hana

The Road to Hana is one of the most iconic and scenic drives in the world, offering an unforgettable journey through Maui's lush rainforests, dramatic coastlines, and cascading waterfalls. Embark on an adventure along the Road to Hana, exploring its various stops and highlighting the unique beauty of each section.

Paia to Keanae

The journey along the Road to Hana begins in the charming town of Paia, located on Maui's north shore. As you set off on this picturesque drive, you'll be greeted by breathtaking coastal views and winding roads that lead you deeper into the heart of Maui.

Leaving Paia, you'll pass by stunning beaches such as Ho'okipa Beach, famous for its powerful waves and world-class windsurfing conditions. As you continue along the road, keep an eye out for the Twin Falls, where you can take a short hike to discover hidden waterfalls and swim in natural pools.

Further along the route, you'll reach the Keanae Peninsula, a stunning coastal area where lush green fields meet the crashing waves of the Pacific Ocean. Keanae is known for its traditional taro farms, where you can learn about the cultivation of this staple crop and sample fresh poi, a traditional Hawaiian dish made from taro root.

Keanae to Hana

As you leave Keanae, the road winds through dense rainforests, offering a sense of seclusion and tranquility. You'll encounter a series of captivating waterfalls, including the iconic Wailua Falls, where you can witness cascades of water plunging into natural pools.

Along this stretch, you'll find the Pua'a Ka'a State Wayside Park, a hidden gem that features multiple waterfalls and swimming holes. Take a refreshing dip in the crystal-clear waters or enjoy a picnic surrounded by the lush tropical scenery.

Continuing on, you'll reach the enchanting Garden of Eden Arboretum, a botanical garden where you can stroll through a collection of rare plants, vibrant flowers, and towering bamboo groves. The garden offers breathtaking viewpoints overlooking the coastline, showcasing the natural splendor of Maui.

Hana and Beyond

Arriving in the town of Hana, you'll be greeted by a charming community and a sense of stepping back in time. Hana is known for its tranquil beaches, rich cultural heritage, and the world-renowned Travaasa Hana Resort, offering a secluded and luxurious retreat.

Explore Hana's beautiful beaches, such as Hamoa Beach, known for its powdery white sands and turquoise waters. Relax under swaying palm trees, swim in the calm waters, or simply take in the serene beauty of the surroundings.

For a deeper immersion into Hawaiian culture, visit the Hana Cultural Center and Museum, where you can learn about the town's history, traditions, and the importance of preserving the local heritage. Hana is also home to the Kahanu Garden, a National Tropical Botanical Garden that showcases indigenous plants and the iconic Pi'ilanihale Heiau, one of the largest ancient temples in Hawaii.

Beyond Hana, the Road to Hana continues to reveal its wonders. Explore the lush landscapes and hidden gems of the Kipahulu District in Haleakala National Park, where you can hike the Pipiwai Trail, admire the cascading Waimoku Falls, and swim in the pools of 'Ohe'o.

As you venture farther along the road, you'll encounter breathtaking coastal views and scenic vistas, such as the stunning black sand beach of Wai'anapanapa State Park. Explore the volcanic caves, hike along the coastline, or simply revel in the awe-inspiring beauty of this unique destination.

Waterfalls and Pools

Seven Sacred Pools (Ohe'o Gulch)

Located in the Kipahulu District of Haleakala National Park, the Seven Sacred Pools, also known as Ohe'o Gulch, is a collection of tiered pools and waterfalls that create a magical oasis. The pools are fed by freshwater streams flowing from the mountains, providing a refreshing and picturesque setting.

As you explore the Seven Sacred Pools, take a dip in the crystal-clear waters and bask in the tranquility of the surroundings. The pools are connected by gentle cascades, allowing visitors to move from one pool to another and discover hidden spots for relaxation. Please note that swimming may be prohibited during certain times due to changing conditions, so always check with park officials before entering the water.

To fully appreciate the beauty of the area, take a short hike along the Pipiwai Trail. This 4-mile round-trip trail leads you through a lush bamboo forest, past towering banyan trees, and culminates at the mesmerizing Waimoku Falls.

Waimoku Falls

Standing at an impressive height of 400 feet, Waimoku Falls is a majestic waterfall that captivates all who visit. The waterfall is the highlight of the Pipiwai Trail in Haleakala National Park's Kipahulu District. The trail itself is a journey through a tropical paradise, with dense foliage, bamboo groves, and a serene atmosphere.

As you hike along the trail, you'll be immersed in the sounds of nature, with birdsong and the rustling of leaves accompanying your journey. After approximately 2 miles, you'll reach the base of Waimoku Falls, where you can witness the awe-inspiring sight of water cascading down the cliff face. Be prepared to be sprayed with mist as you get closer to the falls, adding to the immersive experience.

Please exercise caution when approaching Waimoku Falls, as the rocks can be slippery. Admire the falls from a safe distance and take in the grandeur of nature's masterpiece.

Twin Falls

Twin Falls is one of the first waterfalls you'll encounter along the Road to Hana, making it a popular stop for travelers embarking on this scenic journey. Located just outside of Paia, Twin Falls offers a taste of Maui's natural beauty without venturing too far from the town.

The falls get their name from the twin cascades that flow into a tranquil pool below. To reach Twin Falls, take a short hike through a picturesque landscape filled with lush greenery and tropical fruit trees. Along the way, you'll pass by vibrant flowers, bamboo groves, and smaller waterfalls, creating a serene and enchanting ambiance.

After the hike, cool off in the refreshing pool beneath Twin Falls, taking in the peaceful surroundings and the gentle sound of falling water. This spot is also a great place for a picnic, allowing you to relax and soak up the beauty of the area.

Wailua Falls

Located on Maui's northeastern side, Wailua Falls is a stunning, multi-tiered waterfall that tumbles down a sheer cliff face. This iconic waterfall is easily accessible, making it a popular attraction for visitors exploring the Road to Hana.

As you approach Wailua Falls, you'll be greeted by the sight of water plunging approximately 80 feet into a tranquil pool below. The mist created by the falls often creates a beautiful rainbow, adding to the allure of this natural wonder. The viewing area provides a vantage point where you can marvel at the sheer power and beauty of the waterfall.

Wailua Falls is best viewed from a distance, as the area near the falls is steep and can be dangerous. Take in the breathtaking scene, capture memorable photos, and appreciate the raw beauty of this majestic waterfall.

Other Maui's Natural Wonders

Iao Valley State Park

Nestled in the lush West Maui Mountains, Iao Valley State Park is a verdant paradise with a rich cultural and historical significance. The park is home to the iconic Iao Needle, a 1,200-foot tall peak that juts out from the valley floor. This towering rock formation holds great spiritual significance in Hawaiian history and is considered a sacred place.

Visitors to Iao Valley State Park can embark on the Iao Valley Trail, which winds through the park's tropical rainforest and offers stunning views of the valley and the Iao Needle. Along the trail, interpretive signs provide information about the area's natural and cultural history.

The park's beauty extends beyond the Iao Needle, with lush greenery, vibrant flowers, and cascading waterfalls that create a serene and picturesque setting. Exploring the park's various viewpoints and trails allows visitors to immerse themselves in the natural wonders of Maui and experience the tranquility of this sacred valley.

As with any natural area, it's important to respect and preserve the delicate ecosystems of Haleakala National Park and Iao Valley State Park. Follow designated trails, pack out any trash, and adhere to any regulations or guidelines provided by park authorities.

Molokini Crater

Situated off the coast of Maui, Molokini Crater is a crescent-shaped volcanic crater that serves as a world-renowned snorkeling and diving destination. This partially submerged volcanic cone is a marine sanctuary, providing an abundance of marine life and crystal-clear waters for visitors to explore.

Embarking on a boat trip to Molokini Crater, you'll have the opportunity to snorkel or dive in the vibrant coral reefs teeming with tropical fish, sea turtles, and even the occasional reef shark. The protected waters of the crater offer excellent visibility, making it an ideal spot for underwater photography and observing the fascinating marine ecosystem.

Whether you're an experienced diver or a beginner snorkeler, Molokini Crater offers an unforgettable adventure and the chance to witness the colorful wonders of Maui's underwater world.

Bamboo Forest

Nestled within Haleakala National Park's Kipahulu District, the Bamboo Forest is a magical and serene place that feels like stepping into a fairytale. As you venture along the Pipiwai Trail, you'll enter a lush bamboo grove that transports you to a different realm.

The towering bamboo stalks create a dense canopy overhead, casting dappled sunlight on the forest floor. Walking through the bamboo-lined path, you'll be mesmerized by the rustling of the leaves, creating a soothing symphony of nature. The unique ambiance and ethereal beauty of the Bamboo Forest make it a favorite spot for photographers and nature enthusiasts.

The Pipiwai Trail continues beyond the Bamboo Forest, leading you to the awe-inspiring Waimoku Falls, as mentioned earlier in Chapter 5. This combination of the Bamboo Forest and Waimoku Falls creates a truly enchanting and unforgettable hiking experience.

Waihee Ridge Trail

The Waihee Ridge Trail is a scenic and invigorating hike that takes you through the lush landscapes of the West Maui Mountains. Located in the Waihee Valley, this trail offers breathtaking panoramic views of Maui's coastline, valleys, and waterfalls.

The trail starts with a steady incline, leading you through a forested area of native Hawaiian plants and colorful flowers. As you ascend, the vegetation changes, and you'll be rewarded with stunning vistas of the surrounding valleys and the sparkling ocean beyond. On a clear day, you can even see neighboring islands in the distance.

At the summit of the trail, you'll be greeted by the sight of the Waihee Valley stretching out before you, a picturesque scene of verdant beauty. Take a moment to savor the tranquility and enjoy a well-deserved break, soaking in the panoramic views.

The Waihee Ridge Trail is considered a moderately challenging hike, with uneven terrain and sections that can be muddy. Proper footwear, plenty of water, and sun protection are essential. Hiking this trail allows you to connect with nature, appreciate Maui's stunning landscapes, and witness the allure of the West Maui Mountains.

West Maui Mountains

The West Maui Mountains, also known as Mauna Kahalawai, are a majestic range that spans the western side of Maui. This ancient volcano has shaped the landscape over millions of years, creating dramatic valleys, sharp ridges, and lush rainforests.

Driving along the scenic Kahekili Highway, you'll be treated to breathtaking views of the mountains' towering peaks and verdant slopes. The road winds through deep valleys and offers numerous lookout points where you can stop and admire the panoramic vistas. The rugged beauty of the West Maui Mountains is a sight to behold, with its rugged cliffs, cascading waterfalls, and vibrant foliage.

One popular destination within the West Maui Mountains is the Iao Valley State Park, as mentioned earlier This park is home to the iconic Iao Needle, a towering rock formation that holds great cultural significance in Hawaiian history.

Exploring the West Maui Mountains provides a unique opportunity to witness the island's geological wonders and immerse yourself in the untamed beauty of Maui's rugged terrain. The ever-changing landscapes and stunning vistas make the journey through the West Maui Mountains a truly unforgettable experience.

CHAPTER 5

Adventures and Outdoor Activities

Maui is not only known for its stunning landscapes but also for the plethora of adventurous and outdoor activities it offers. Explore some of the island's most popular activities, including surfing, stand-up paddleboarding, and the best spots to enjoy these exhilarating water sports.

Surfing and Stand-Up Paddleboarding

Surfing and stand-up paddleboarding are iconic water sports that allow visitors to immerse themselves in Maui's vibrant coastal culture while riding the island's legendary waves. Whether you're a seasoned surfer or a beginner looking to catch your first wave, Maui offers a variety of spots that cater to different skill levels.

Ho'okipa Beach

Ho'okipa Beach, located on Maui's northern coast, is renowned as a world-class windsurfing and surfing destination. This iconic beach attracts professional surfers and windsurfers from around the globe who come to tackle the powerful waves and harness the strong trade winds.

Surfers of all levels can find a challenge at Ho'okipa Beach. Experienced surfers often head to the outer reef, where larger swells provide thrilling rides. Beginners can stick to the inside breaks, which offer smaller waves and a more forgiving learning environment. The beach itself is a hub of activity, with surfers riding the waves, windsurfers performing acrobatics, and spectators enjoying the incredible skills on display.

Honolua Bay

Located on Maui's northwest coast, Honolua Bay is a legendary surf spot known for its pristine conditions and world-class waves. Surrounded by a lush marine reserve, Honolua Bay offers a unique and picturesque setting for surfers and stand-up paddleboarders.

Honolua Bay is famous for its powerful and consistent winter swells that create barreling waves, attracting experienced surfers seeking an adrenaline rush. During the summer months, the bay transforms into a peaceful haven with smaller waves, making it an ideal spot for beginners or those looking to enjoy a leisurely paddle.

Beyond the exceptional surfing and stand-up paddleboarding opportunities, Honolua Bay is also known for its vibrant marine life. Snorkelers can explore the vibrant coral reefs teeming with colorful fish and other marine creatures, creating an unforgettable underwater adventure.

Launiupoko Beach Park

Launiupoko Beach Park, located just south of Lahaina, offers a family-friendly environment for both surfing and stand-up paddleboarding. The beach park features a shallow and sandy bottom, making it an ideal spot for beginners to learn and practice these water sports.

The gentle waves at Launiupoko Beach Park are perfect for beginners to catch their first rides on a surfboard or paddle out on a stand-up paddleboard. The park provides ample space for families to set up picnic areas, relax under the shade of palm trees, and watch as surfers and paddleboarders enjoy the waves.

Lessons and equipment rentals are available at nearby surf schools, allowing visitors to receive professional instruction and get all the necessary gear for a safe and enjoyable experience on the water.

Engaging in surfing or stand-up paddleboarding on Maui allows you to connect with the island's vibrant ocean culture, challenge yourself physically, and experience the thrill of riding the waves. Whether you're a seasoned surfer or a curious beginner, Maui offers a variety of spots to cater to different skill levels, ensuring an unforgettable adventure in the island's sparkling waters.

Hiking and Trails

Pipiwai Trail

The Pipiwai Trail, located in Haleakala National Park's Kipahulu District, is a 4-mile round-trip hike that takes you on a mesmerizing journey through a tropical wonderland. This iconic trail showcases some of Maui's most enchanting features, including a bamboo forest, towering waterfalls, and a majestic final destination.

As you begin the hike, you'll enter a lush bamboo grove, where towering bamboo stalks create a surreal and serene atmosphere. The sound of rustling leaves and the filtered sunlight create a magical ambiance as you make your way through this unique section of the trail.

Continuing along the path, you'll be greeted by the sight of Makahiku Falls, a stunning 185-foot waterfall that cascades down a lush cliff face. Take a moment to savor the beauty of this natural masterpiece and feel the refreshing mist created by the falls.

The journey culminates at the awe-inspiring Waimoku Falls, a towering waterfall that stands at approximately 400 feet. As you approach the falls, you'll be captivated by its grandeur and the thundering sound of water crashing into the pool below. Be prepared for a refreshing mist as you get closer to this magnificent display of nature's power.

Throughout the hike, informative signage provides insights into the local flora, fauna, and cultural significance of the area, enhancing your connection to the surroundings. The Pipiwai Trail is a moderately challenging hike, with some steep sections and uneven terrain. Proper footwear, plenty of water, and sun protection are essential for an enjoyable experience.

Waihou Spring Trail

The Waihou Spring Trail, located in the upcountry region of Maui, offers a tranquil escape into a lush forested area filled with native Hawaiian plants and cool, refreshing air. This hidden gem is an ideal choice for those seeking a serene hiking experience away from the more crowded tourist areas.

As you embark on the Waihou Spring Trail, you'll be greeted by the soothing sounds of flowing water and the fragrance of eucalyptus trees. The trail follows a gentle path, leading you through a dense forest filled with endemic flora and vibrant greenery.

Along the way, you'll encounter the Waihou Spring, a natural spring that provides fresh water to the surrounding area. Take a moment to appreciate the serene beauty of the spring and listen to the peaceful symphony of nature.

The Waihou Spring Trail offers a peaceful environment for reflection and connection with nature. As you stroll along the trail, you may encounter native birds and other wildlife, adding to the sense of immersion in Maui's natural wonders.

Sliding Sands Trail

For those seeking a more challenging hiking experience, the Sliding Sands Trail in Haleakala National Park's Summit District is a must-visit destination. This trail takes you into the heart of the volcanic crater, offering a surreal and otherworldly landscape unlike anything else on the island.

As you descend into the crater, you'll be surrounded by vast stretches of barren volcanic terrain, with colorful cinder cones dotting the landscape. The desolate yet awe-inspiring scenery creates a sense of adventure and exploration.

The Sliding Sands Trail allows hikers to venture as far as their time and energy permit, with options for shorter hikes or longer treks that can last several hours. The trail offers opportunities to witness unique geological features, such as the famous silversword plants, which are endemic to Haleakala and can be found nowhere else on Earth.

It's important to note that hiking in the crater presents its own set of challenges. The high elevation, exposure to the elements, and rapidly changing weather conditions require proper preparation and caution. Dress in layers, bring ample water, and be mindful of your physical abilities and the signs of altitude sickness.

Exploring Maui's hiking trails allows you to connect with the island's natural beauty, witness breathtaking landscapes, and discover hidden gems tucked away in its diverse ecosystems. Whether you choose the enchanting Pipiwai Trail, the tranquil Waihou Spring Trail, or the rugged adventure of the Sliding Sands Trail, each hiking experience on Maui is sure to leave you with unforgettable memories and a deeper appreciation for the island's natural wonders.

Ziplining

Maui's lush landscapes and breathtaking views make it an ideal destination for ziplining, providing a unique perspective on the island's natural beauty. Soar through the air and experience the exhilaration of flying over canopies, valleys, and waterfalls while enjoying panoramic vistas of the island.

Skyline Eco-Adventures

Skyline Eco-Adventures offers an exhilarating ziplining experience that combines thrilling rides with a focus on environmental stewardship. With multiple zipline courses, including the Haleakala and Ka'anapali lines, you'll have the opportunity to zip through towering eucalyptus forests, soar above scenic valleys, and catch glimpses of cascading waterfalls.

As you glide through the air, trained guides will share their knowledge of Maui's unique ecosystems and provide insights into the island's rich cultural heritage. Skyline Eco-Adventures ensures a safe and eco-friendly experience, allowing you to appreciate Maui's natural beauty from a completely new perspective.

Piiholo Ranch Zipline

Located in Upcountry Maui, Piiholo Ranch Zipline offers an exhilarating adventure in a picturesque setting. With ziplines that crisscross the ranch's sprawling landscapes, you'll have the opportunity to take in panoramic views of the ocean, mountains, and Maui's scenic beauty.

The zipline courses at Piiholo Ranch cater to all levels of experience, from beginners to adrenaline seekers. Soar through the air, fly over lush canyons, and feel the rush of adrenaline as you take in the stunning surroundings.

Whether you choose Skyline Eco-Adventures or Piiholo Ranch Zipline, ziplining on Maui offers a thrilling and unique way to explore the island's natural wonders. So, strap in, embrace the excitement, and enjoy the bird's-eye view of Maui's breathtaking landscapes.

Snorkeling and Scuba Diving

Maui's crystal-clear waters are teeming with vibrant marine life and breathtaking underwater ecosystems. Snorkeling and scuba diving offer the opportunity to explore Maui's coral reefs, encounter colorful fish, and witness the beauty of the underwater world.

Molokini Crater

Molokini Crater, mentioned earlier is not only a fantastic snorkeling spot but also a popular destination for scuba diving. Its pristine waters, thriving coral reefs, and abundant marine life make it a must-visit site for underwater enthusiasts.

Plunge into the turquoise waters and discover a vibrant underwater world filled with tropical fish, sea turtles, and an array of coral species. The clear visibility and calm conditions make Molokini Crater an ideal location for both beginner and experienced snorkelers and divers.

Honolua Bay Marine Preserve

Honolua Bay Marine Preserve, mentioned earlier, is another fantastic location for snorkeling and diving on Maui. This protected bay offers crystal-clear waters, abundant marine life, and stunning coral formations.

As you explore the underwater realm of Honolua Bay, you'll encounter schools of colorful fish, graceful sea turtles, and even the occasional reef shark. The bay's calm and sheltered conditions provide an ideal environment for snorkelers and divers of all skill levels to enjoy Maui's marine treasures.

Black Rock (Pu'u Keka'a)

Located on Ka'anapali Beach, Black Rock, also known as Pu'u Keka'a, is a popular snorkeling spot where you can encounter a variety of marine life and explore the vibrant underwater world of Maui.

Black Rock's rocky outcrop provides a habitat for an abundance of fish and coral, creating an underwater playground for snorkelers. Swim alongside tropical fish, marvel at the coral formations, and keep an eye out for the occasional Hawaiian green sea turtle that frequents the area.

Golfing in Maui

Maui is home to world-class golf courses that offer stunning views, challenging fairways, and an unforgettable golfing experience. With a combination of lush greens, ocean vistas, and dramatic landscapes, Maui's golf courses attract players from around the world.

Kapalua Golf Course

The Kapalua Golf Course, located on Maui's west coast, is a premier golfing destination known for its stunning views and championship-caliber courses. With two courses, the Plantation Course and the Bay Course, Kapalua offers a golfing experience that combines natural beauty with challenging fairways.

Wailea Golf Club

Situated on Maui's sunny southern coast, the Wailea Golf Club is home to three distinct courses: the Gold Course, the Emerald Course, and the Blue Course. Each course offers breathtaking ocean views, immaculate greens, and unique challenges, ensuring a memorable golfing experience.

Golfing in Maui allows you to enjoy the island's natural beauty while testing your skills on world-class courses. Whether you're a seasoned golfer or a beginner, Maui's golf courses provide a remarkable combination of sport, relaxation, and scenic splendor.

Kayaking and Canoeing

Maui's calm bays and pristine coastlines offer ideal conditions for kayaking and canoeing. Paddle along the shoreline, explore hidden coves, and witness the beauty of Maui's coastal landscapes from a different perspective.

Whether you choose to embark on a guided kayak tour or rent a kayak or canoe and explore at your own pace, you'll have the opportunity to immerse yourself in the tranquility of Maui's waters and discover secluded spots that can only be accessed by boat.

Whale Watching

Maui's warm waters are a haven for humpback whales during their annual migration from Alaska. Whale watching is a popular activity that allows visitors to witness these majestic creatures up close and personal, providing a once-in-a-lifetime experience.

From December to April, humpback whales make their way to Maui's waters to breed, give birth, and nurse their young. Join a whale-watching excursion and embark on a thrilling adventure as you spot these magnificent creatures breaching, tail-slapping, and performing acrobatic displays.

As you sail along Maui's coast, knowledgeable naturalists will provide fascinating insights into the behaviors and characteristics of humpback whales, enhancing your understanding and appreciation of these gentle giants.

CHAPTER 6

Exploring Maui's Underwater World

Maui's underwater world is a vibrant and mesmerizing ecosystem teeming with diverse marine life, colorful coral reefs, and captivating underwater landscapes. dive into the depths of Maui's oceans and explore the fascinating marine life, discover top snorkeling spots, delve into the thrilling world of scuba diving, embark on sailing and catamaran tours, experience submarine adventures, and learn about responsible ocean practices that help protect this fragile ecosystem.

Marine Life and Coral Reefs

Maui's waters are home to a rich diversity of marine life, offering visitors a chance to encounter remarkable creatures and witness the delicate balance of the ocean ecosystem.

Sea Turtles

One of the most iconic marine creatures found in Maui's waters is the Hawaiian green sea turtle, also known as honu. These gentle giants can often be spotted gracefully gliding through the ocean or basking on the sandy shores. Snorkelers and divers are fortunate to witness these magnificent creatures up close, as they gracefully swim among the coral reefs. Remember to observe sea turtles from a respectful distance and never touch or disturb them, as they are protected by law.

Spinner Dolphins

Maui's waters are also frequented by spinner dolphins, which are known for their acrobatic displays and playful nature. These intelligent creatures often travel in pods, leaping and spinning in the air, captivating onlookers. Encountering a pod of spinner dolphins while snorkeling, diving, or during a boat excursion is an incredible experience that will leave you in awe of their agility and beauty.

Tropical Fish

Maui's coral reefs are home to a dazzling array of tropical fish, each adding their unique colors and patterns to the underwater tapestry. Snorkelers and divers will have the opportunity to swim alongside vibrant schools of fish, such as butterflyfish, angelfish, parrotfish, and many more. The kaleidoscope of colors and the graceful movements of these fish create a magical underwater spectacle that will leave you captivated.

Snorkeling Spots

Maui offers a myriad of exceptional snorkeling spots that allow visitors to explore the beauty of the island's underwater world.

Molokini Crater

Molokini Crater, mentioned earlier, is not only a fantastic spot for scuba diving but also an excellent destination for snorkelers. The crystal-clear waters surrounding the partially submerged volcanic cone provide incredible visibility and a chance to witness an abundance of marine life. Snorkelers can explore vibrant coral reefs, encounter tropical fish, and even spot sea turtles gliding through the waters.

Honolua Bay

Honolua Bay, mentioned earlier, is a marine preserve located on Maui's northwest coast. This protected bay offers some of the best snorkeling opportunities on the island. The bay's calm and clear waters are ideal for snorkelers of all levels, allowing them to observe a variety of fish species and witness the beauty of the coral reefs. The abundance of marine life in Honolua Bay makes it a must-visit snorkeling spot for nature enthusiasts.

Ahihi-Kinau Natural Area Reserve

Located on Maui's southern coast, the Ahihi-Kinau Natural Area Reserve is a pristine marine environment that offers exceptional snorkeling experiences. The reserve's lava rock formations create a unique underwater landscape, providing shelter to a diverse array of marine species. Snorkelers can swim alongside colorful fish, explore vibrant coral gardens, and immerse themselves in the tranquility of this protected marine sanctuary.

Scuba Diving

For those seeking a more immersive experience in Maui's underwater world, scuba diving offers the opportunity to explore the depths of the ocean and witness its hidden treasures.

Cathedrals at Lanai

A short boat ride from Maui's shores will take you to the neighboring island of Lanai, where the Cathedrals stand as one of the most renowned dive sites in Hawaii. The Cathedrals are a series of underwater lava tubes that have formed beautiful caverns with stunning light effects. Divers can explore these caverns, observing the intricate formations and encountering marine life such as nudibranchs, eels, and colorful reef fish.

Molokini Back Wall

Beyond the Molokini Crater's crescent-shaped rim lies the Molokini Back Wall, a thrilling dive site that drops down to great depths. This vertical wall is adorned with vibrant corals, sponges, and sea fans, offering an awe-inspiring sight for divers. Along the wall, pelagic species such as sharks, rays, and schools of fish can often be spotted, creating an unforgettable underwater encounter.

Mala Wharf

The Mala Wharf, located near Lahaina, is an artificial reef formed by the remains of an old pier. This unique dive site is home to a variety of marine life, including colorful reef fish, eels, and even octopuses. Exploring the Mala Wharf allows divers to witness the resilience of nature as it reclaims this man-made structure, creating a thriving ecosystem that divers can appreciate.

Sailing and Catamaran Tours

To experience Maui's underwater world from a different perspective, embark on a sailing or catamaran tour that combines the joy of sailing with the opportunity for snorkeling or simply admiring the beauty of the coastline.

Sailing and catamaran tours offer a relaxing and scenic way to explore Maui's shores. Feel the wind in your hair as you glide across the ocean, taking in breathtaking views of the coastline and the vast expanse of the Pacific. These tours often include stops at prime snorkeling spots, allowing you to don your gear and plunge into the crystal-clear waters to discover the wonders beneath the surface.

Submarine Tours

For those who prefer to explore Maui's underwater world without getting wet, submarine tours provide a unique and immersive experience. Descend into the depths of the ocean aboard a submarine and witness the captivating marine life and coral reefs from the comfort of a viewing window.

Submarine tours offer a close-up look at Maui's underwater landscapes and provide an opportunity to learn about the marine ecosystem from knowledgeable guides. Marvel at the vibrant coral formations, observe tropical fish as they swim by, and perhaps even spot sea turtles or other marine creatures as they gracefully glide through the water.

Responsible Ocean Practices

As visitors to Maui's underwater world, it is crucial to engage in responsible ocean practices to ensure the preservation of this fragile ecosystem for generations to come.

When snorkeling or diving, avoid touching or damaging coral reefs, as they are delicate and take years to grow. Respect the marine life by observing from a distance and never feeding or harassing the animals. Use reef-safe sunscreen to protect your skin without harming the coral reefs. Dispose of any waste properly and never litter on land or at sea.

Support local conservation efforts and organizations that work to protect Maui's marine ecosystem. Participate in beach cleanups and educate others about the importance of preserving the ocean environment.

By adopting responsible ocean practices, you become an advocate for the health and preservation of Maui's underwater world, ensuring that future generations can continue to explore and appreciate its remarkable beauty.

CHAPTER 7

Cultural Immersion

Maui's rich cultural heritage offers visitors a chance to immerse themselves in the traditions, arts, and customs of the island. Explore the vibrant world of cultural immersion, from attending a traditional Hawaiian luau to visiting ancient temples and sacred sites. We'll also discover the artistic expressions of Maui through its art and crafts scene and experience the soul-stirring melodies of Hawaiian music and dance.

Hawaiian Luau

A Hawaiian luau is a festive celebration that showcases the cultural traditions, music, dance, and culinary delights of the islands. Attending a luau is a wonderful way to experience the spirit of aloha and immerse yourself in Hawaiian hospitality.

As you enter the luau grounds, you'll be greeted with a warm aloha and adorned with a beautiful lei, a symbol of welcome and friendship. Feast on traditional Hawaiian dishes such as kalua pig (slow-cooked in an underground imu oven), poi (a staple food made from taro), lomi lomi salmon, and haupia (coconut pudding).

During the luau, you'll be treated to captivating performances of hula, showcasing the graceful movements and storytelling elements of this ancient dance form. The sound of live music, the swaying of palm trees, and the vibrant colors of traditional costumes create an unforgettable atmosphere of cultural celebration.

Ancient Temples and Sacred Sites

Maui is home to several ancient temples and sacred sites that offer a glimpse into the island's rich history and spiritual beliefs. Visiting these sacred places allows for a deeper understanding of the cultural significance and reverence attached to these sites.

Hale O Pi'ilani Heiau

Hale O Pi'ilani Heiau, located in the Kahanu Garden in Hana, is one of Maui's most significant ancient temples. This massive stone structure is a testament to the engineering and spiritual prowess of the ancient Hawaiians. Explore the temple grounds, learn about its historical significance, and witness the breathtaking views of the surrounding landscape.

Honokahua Preservation Site

Honokahua Preservation Site, also known as Pu'u Keka'a or Black Rock, is a sacred site located on Ka'anapali Beach in Lahaina. This site holds immense cultural and historical importance as a burial ground and ceremonial site. Visitors can pay their respects and learn about the spiritual significance attached to this revered place.

Lahaina Jodo Mission

The Lahaina Jodo Mission is a Buddhist temple located in Lahaina, offering a unique cultural experience on the island. Admire the beautiful architecture and serene gardens of the temple while learning about the history and practices of Buddhism in Hawaii. Take part in traditional ceremonies and gain insight into the island's multicultural heritage.

Art and Crafts

Maui's art and crafts scene is a vibrant reflection of the island's creativity and cultural expressions. From traditional crafts to contemporary artwork, exploring Maui's artistic offerings allows for a deeper connection to the island's cultural tapestry.

Maui Crafts Guild

The Maui Crafts Guild, located in Paia, is a cooperative of local artisans dedicated to preserving and promoting traditional craftsmanship. Browse through the gallery and discover unique creations such as handcrafted jewelry, pottery, textiles, woodwork, and more. Engaging with the artists and learning about their techniques adds an enriching dimension to the experience.

Hui No'eau Visual Arts Center

The Hui No'eau Visual Arts Center, situated in Upcountry Maui, is a hub for creativity and artistic expression. The center offers a variety of exhibitions, workshops, and events that showcase the work of local and visiting artists. Explore the galleries, participate in a class, or attend an art talk to gain a deeper understanding of Maui's artistic community.

Maui Hands Gallery

The Maui Hands Gallery has multiple locations across the island, providing a platform for local artists to showcase their work. From paintings and sculptures to ceramics and jewelry, the gallery features an eclectic mix of artistic creations that highlight the diverse talents of Maui's artistic community. Engage with the artists, learn about their inspirations, and take home a unique piece of Maui's creative spirit.

Music and Dance

Music and dance are integral components of Hawaiian culture, allowing for the expression of stories, emotions, and traditions. Engaging with the melodic rhythms and graceful movements of Hawaiian music and dance is a powerful way to connect with the island's cultural heritage.

Ukulele and Hula

The ukulele, a small guitar-like instrument, is synonymous with Hawaiian music. Attend a ukulele performance and be mesmerized by the sweet melodies and joyful strumming. Hula, the traditional dance form of Hawaii, tells stories through graceful movements and gestures. Experience the beauty and grace of hula by attending a performance or even participating in a hula class to learn the basic steps and hand motions.

Slack Key Guitar

Slack key guitar is a unique Hawaiian music style characterized by the fingerpicking technique and open tunings. Experience the soulful melodies of slack key guitar by attending a live performance or immersing yourself in the soothing sounds of slack key guitar albums that capture the essence of Hawaii's musical heritage.

Maui Arts and Cultural Center

The Maui Arts and Cultural Center, located in Kahului, hosts a variety of performances and events that celebrate Hawaiian music, dance, and performing arts. From traditional hula shows to contemporary musical performances, the center provides a platform for local artists to showcase their talents and for visitors to engage with Maui's cultural offerings.

CHAPTER 8

Dining and Cuisine

Maui's culinary scene is a delightful fusion of traditional Hawaiian flavors, local food trucks and shacks, fine dining establishments, farm-to-table experiences, and unique culinary adventures. In this chapter, we will indulge our taste buds and explore the diverse array of dining options that await on the island.

Traditional Hawaiian Flavors

Immerse yourself in the rich tapestry of traditional Hawaiian flavors, which draw inspiration from the island's bountiful land and sea. From poi (a staple made from taro) to kalua pig (slow-roasted in an underground imu oven), traditional Hawaiian dishes offer a unique taste of the island's cultural heritage. Seek out local eateries and restaurants that showcase these authentic flavors, allowing you to savor the true essence of Hawaii.

Local Food Trucks and Shacks

For a taste of casual and authentic local cuisine, Maui's food trucks and shacks are the perfect go-to spots. These hidden gems offer a diverse range of mouthwatering dishes influenced by various culinary traditions. Whether you're craving plate lunches, fresh seafood, poke bowls, or shave ice, the local food trucks and shacks serve up delicious and affordable options that will satisfy any palate.

Fine Dining and Upscale Restaurants

Maui is home to a plethora of fine dining establishments and upscale restaurants that showcase the island's culinary prowess. From award-winning chefs to breathtaking oceanfront locations, these venues offer a memorable dining experience for those seeking refined flavors and impeccable service. Indulge in innovative dishes featuring locally sourced ingredients, and allow the artistry of the chefs to take you on a gastronomic journey through Maui's flavors.

Farm-to-Table Experiences

Maui's fertile land and commitment to sustainability have given rise to a thriving farm-to-table movement. Numerous restaurants and eateries embrace the concept of sourcing ingredients directly from local farmers, ensuring the freshest and highest quality produce on their menus. Immerse yourself in the farm-to-table experience, where you can savor dishes crafted with ingredients harvested just moments away. This culinary approach not only supports local farmers but also allows you to taste the true essence of Maui's agricultural abundance.

Unique Culinary Experiences

Maui offers a range of unique culinary experiences that showcase the island's diverse offerings and creative talents.

Maui Winery

The Maui Winery, located in Ulupalakua, invites visitors to indulge in the flavors of Maui's wines. Explore the vineyards, learn about the winemaking process, and sample a variety of handcrafted wines, including pineapple wine and traditional grape varietals. Immerse yourself in the enchanting atmosphere of the winery and raise a glass to the island's terroir.

Maui Brewing Company

Beer enthusiasts will delight in a visit to the Maui Brewing Company. Take a tour of the brewery, learn about the brewing process, and sample a wide selection of locally crafted beers. From refreshing ales to bold stouts, the Maui Brewing Company offers a range of flavors that capture the essence of the island. Cheers to the art of craft brewing and the spirit of aloha!

Hali'imaile General Store

The Hali'imaile General Store, located in Upcountry Maui, is a renowned restaurant that marries flavors from around the world with the island's local ingredients. Created by Chef Beverly Gannon, this iconic eatery offers a unique blend of Hawaiian, Asian, and European influences, resulting in innovative and flavorful dishes. Immerse yourself in the vibrant ambiance of the general store and savor the culinary creations that have made it a beloved culinary destination.

CHAPTER 9

Shopping and Souvenirs

Maui offers a delightful shopping experience, with a wide array of options to find unique souvenirs, locally made crafts, island-produced goods, and stylish Hawaiian clothing and accessories. Explore the shopping districts, markets, and boutiques where you can discover treasures to commemorate your visit to the island.

Shopping Districts and Centers

Maui boasts several shopping districts and centers that offer a diverse range of shops, boutiques, and eateries, creating a one-stop destination for all your shopping needs.

Whether you're strolling through Lahaina's Front Street, exploring the bustling Whalers Village in Ka'anapali, or perusing the upscale shops of Wailea, you'll find an abundance of options for fashion, jewelry, art, and more. These vibrant shopping districts provide a lively atmosphere and a variety of choices, making them ideal destinations for finding that perfect souvenir.

Local Markets and Flea Markets

For an authentic Maui shopping experience, immerse yourself in the local markets and flea markets where you can find unique treasures, local produce, handmade crafts, and much more.

Visit the Maui Swap Meet, held every Saturday at the University of Hawaii Maui College in Kahului. This large flea market features a wide range of vendors offering everything from fresh produce and clothing to handmade crafts and artwork. Explore the stalls, engage with local artisans, and discover hidden gems that reflect the island's cultural heritage.

Hawaiian Clothing and Accessories

Embrace the spirit of aloha and the island lifestyle by browsing through the vibrant selection of Hawaiian clothing and accessories available on Maui.

From traditional aloha shirts (known as "Hawaiian shirts") and muumuus to stylish dresses and sarongs, there are options to suit every taste and occasion. Look for locally designed and made clothing that showcases

Hawaiian motifs and patterns, allowing you to take a piece of the island's fashion culture home with you.

Don't forget to complement your outfit with accessories such as handcrafted hats, sandals, and locally inspired jewelry featuring elements like sea turtles, hibiscus flowers, or plumeria blossoms. These accessories not only add a touch of Hawaiian flair to your ensemble but also serve as lasting reminders of your time in Maui.

Handmade Crafts and Artwork

Maui's vibrant artistic community offers an array of handmade crafts and artwork that capture the island's natural beauty and cultural expressions.

Explore galleries and artisan shops to discover one-of-a-kind pieces created by local artists. From ceramics and glasswork to wood carvings and textiles, you'll find a diverse range of crafts that reflect the creativity and skill of Maui's artisans. Admire the intricate details, learn about the artistic processes, and select a piece that resonates with you, serving as a tangible memory of your Maui experience.

Island-Produced Goods and Food

Maui is known for its locally produced goods and flavorful food products that highlight the island's agricultural abundance and culinary traditions.

Look for specialty food items such as Maui coffee, macadamia nuts, tropical fruit preserves, and locally made chocolates. These delectable treats not only make excellent souvenirs but also allow you to savor the unique flavors of Maui long after your visit.

Additionally, explore island-produced goods such as natural skincare products made with local ingredients, including coconut oil and tropical botanicals. These products offer a way to pamper yourself while supporting local businesses committed to sustainable and eco-friendly practices.

Jewelry and Pearls

Maui is renowned for its exquisite jewelry, including stunning pieces crafted with pearls and other precious gemstones.

Explore jewelry stores and boutiques that offer a range of designs, from traditional Hawaiian motifs to contemporary styles. Consider investing in a beautiful pearl necklace, bracelet, or pair of earrings, as pearls are a symbol of elegance and timeless beauty. Choose from a variety of colors, shapes, and sizes to find the perfect piece that captures the allure of Maui's ocean treasures.

CHAPTER 10

Accommodations and Luxury Resorts

Luxury Resorts and Hotels

Maui is renowned for its world-class luxury resorts and hotels that provide exceptional service, stunning views, and an array of amenities. Let's explore some of the top luxury resorts on the island:

Wailea Resorts

Wailea is a premier resort destination on Maui's south coast, known for its pristine beaches, championship golf courses, and upscale accommodations. The luxury resorts in Wailea offer a blend of elegance and relaxation, with spacious rooms, private lanais (balconies), exquisite dining options, rejuvenating spas, and meticulously manicured grounds. Enjoy access to pools, beachfront locations, and world-class amenities that cater to your every need.

Kaanapali Resorts

Located on Maui's northwest coast, Kaanapali is famous for its golden sandy beaches and vibrant oceanfront atmosphere. The luxury resorts in Kaanapali offer a mix of modern sophistication and Hawaiian charm. Experience lavish accommodations with ocean views, indulge in fine dining experiences, relax by infinity pools, and pamper yourself with spa treatments. Take advantage of the resort's proximity to Whalers Village, where you can shop, dine, and experience the lively atmosphere.

Kapalua Resorts

Nestled on Maui's northwest shore, Kapalua is a secluded and picturesque area known for its championship golf courses, stunning coastal trails, and unspoiled beauty. The luxury resorts in Kapalua provide a serene retreat amidst lush greenery and breathtaking ocean views. Enjoy upscale accommodations with elegant touches, dine at award-winning restaurants, rejuvenate at world-class spas, and take advantage of exclusive access to Kapalua's pristine beaches.

Boutique Hotels and Inns

For those seeking a more intimate and personalized experience, Maui offers a selection of boutique hotels and inns that capture the island's charm and hospitality.

Boutique hotels and inns provide unique accommodations with a focus on individualized service and attention to detail. These properties often have a distinct character and offer a more authentic and intimate experience. Enjoy stylishly appointed rooms, personalized concierge services, and a cozy ambiance that creates a home away from home.

Vacation Rentals and Condos

Maui's vacation rentals and condos are a popular choice for travelers seeking flexibility, privacy, and the comforts of a home away from home.

Vacation rentals and condos provide fully furnished accommodations with kitchen facilities, living areas, and often private lanais. Whether you're looking for a beachfront condo, a charming cottage, or a spacious villa, you'll find a wide range of options that cater to different group sizes and budgets. Enjoy the convenience of cooking your own meals, relaxing in comfortable living spaces, and experiencing Maui at your own pace.

Cozy Bed and Breakfasts

Maui's bed and breakfast establishments offer a cozy and intimate experience, often run by local hosts who provide personalized service and insider knowledge about the island.

Stay in charming accommodations nestled in scenic locations, such as Upcountry Maui or along the coast. Wake up to a homemade breakfast featuring local ingredients and start your day with recommendations from your hosts on the best hidden gems and attractions to explore. Bed and breakfasts provide a warm and welcoming atmosphere, creating a sense of community and allowing you to connect with fellow travelers and locals.

Camping and RV Parks

For nature enthusiasts and those seeking a more adventurous experience, Maui offers camping and RV parks that allow you to immerse yourself in the island's natural beauty.

Pitch a tent or park your RV in designated camping areas, where you can wake up to the sound of waves crashing or birds chirping. Enjoy the simplicity of outdoor living while being surrounded by Maui's stunning landscapes. Many camping areas offer facilities such as restrooms, showers, and picnic tables, providing the necessary amenities for a comfortable camping experience.

CHAPTER 11

Insider Tips and Practical Information

Transportation Options

Getting around Maui is essential for exploring the island's diverse attractions. Here are some transportation options to consider:

Car Rentals

Renting a car is a popular choice for travelers who want the freedom to explore Maui at their own pace. Numerous car rental companies operate on the island, offering a range of vehicles to suit different needs and budgets. Be sure to book your car in advance, especially during peak travel seasons.

Public Transportation

Maui's public transportation system, known as the Maui Bus, provides an affordable and convenient way to get around the island. The bus network covers major routes and popular destinations, making it an excellent option for those without a car. However, be aware that bus frequency may vary, so plan your itinerary accordingly.

Biking and Scooter Rentals

For eco-conscious travelers or those looking for a more active way to explore, biking and scooter rentals are available on Maui. These options allow you to navigate through scenic areas and enjoy a unique perspective of the island's beauty. Always follow safety guidelines and wear appropriate protective gear.

Safety Tips and Guidelines

Maui is a relatively safe destination, but it's essential to keep safety in mind during your visit. Here are some tips to ensure a safe and enjoyable experience:

Be cautious when swimming or participating in water activities, as ocean conditions can change quickly. Always follow lifeguard instructions and be mindful of strong currents and wave conditions.

Protect yourself from the sun's rays by wearing sunscreen, a hat, and sunglasses. Stay hydrated and seek shade during the hottest parts of the day.

Respect the natural environment and follow posted signs and regulations when hiking, visiting parks, or engaging in outdoor activities. Be mindful of the fragile ecosystems and wildlife.

Secure your belongings and avoid leaving valuables unattended. Use hotel safes or lock your car when exploring popular tourist areas.

Customs and Etiquette

Respecting local customs and practicing proper etiquette will help you connect with the people of Maui and show appreciation for their culture. Consider the following customs and etiquette tips:

Aloha spirit: Embrace the spirit of aloha, which embodies friendliness, respect, and hospitality. Greet others with a warm "aloha" and be open to the welcoming nature of the locals.

2. Removing shoes: When entering someone's home or certain establishments, it's customary to remove your shoes as a sign of respect.

3. Respect for nature: Hawaiians have a deep reverence for the environment. Practice responsible tourism by avoiding littering, staying on designated paths, and respecting marine life while engaging in activities like snorkeling or swimming.

Language

When planning to explore Maui, it's helpful to familiarize yourself with some useful Hawaiian words and phrases. While English is widely spoken on the island, learning a few key expressions will not only enhance your cultural experience but also show respect for the local language. Here are some essential Hawaiian words and phrases to learn:

1. Aloha - [ah-LOH-hah] - This versatile word is often considered the cornerstone of Hawaiian culture. It can mean "hello," "goodbye," "love," and "affection." It embodies the spirit of warmth, hospitality, and connection.

2. Mahalo - [mah-HAH-loh] - A widely recognized word, mahalo means "thank you." Express your gratitude and appreciation by using this word when someone helps you or provides a service.

3. Ohana - [oh-HAH-nah] - Ohana refers to family, but its meaning extends beyond blood relations. It includes close friends and community, emphasizing the importance of interconnectedness and unity.

4. E Komo Mai - [ay KOH-moh MY] - This phrase translates to "welcome." It's often used to greet visitors and express hospitality. You might hear it upon arriving at a hotel or entering a local establishment.

5. Pau Hana - [pow HAH-nah] - Pau hana refers to the time after work or quitting time. It's a phrase used to indicate relaxation, downtime, and socializing with friends or colleagues.

6. Pono - [POH-noh] - Pono carries the essence of righteousness, balance, and harmony. It emphasizes the importance of living a morally upright and just life.

7. Mahina - [mah-HEE-nah] - Mahina means "moon" in Hawaiian. As the moon plays a significant role in Hawaiian culture, this word can be used to refer to the lunar phase or the moon itself.

8. Makai - [mah-KAI] - Makai means "toward the ocean" or "seaward." It is often used in directions to indicate a location closer to the ocean.

9. Mauka - [MAU-kah] - Mauka means "toward the mountains" or "inland." When giving or receiving directions, this word helps indicate a location closer to the mountains or inland areas.

10. Hana Hou - [HAH-nah HOH] - Literally meaning "do again," hana hou is a phrase used to request an encore. It's commonly used during performances or

events to express the desire for an artist or group to perform again.

Essential Contacts and Emergency Numbers

It's essential to have access to essential contacts and emergency numbers during your stay in Maui. Save these numbers in your phone or keep them handy for quick reference:

Emergency Services: Dial 911 for emergencies requiring police, fire, or medical assistance.

Maui Visitors Bureau: Contact the Maui Visitors Bureau for general information, travel assistance, and recommendations on attractions and activities.

Local Transportation Providers: Keep contact information for car rental agencies, taxi services, and public transportation authorities.

Medical Facilities: Note the locations and contact information of hospitals, urgent care centers, and pharmacies in case of a medical emergency.

Itineraries for Different Types of Travelers

Family-Friendly Itinerary

For families traveling with children, this itinerary is designed to provide a balance of fun, educational, and memorable experiences that cater to the whole family's interests. Explore Maui's beautiful beaches, visit family-oriented attractions, and embark on outdoor adventures suitable for all ages.

Day 1: Arrival and Beach Time
- Upon arrival, settle into your accommodation and take some time to relax at one of Maui's stunning beaches. Ka'anapali Beach or Kapalua Bay Beach are great options for families with calm waters and beautiful scenery. Let the kids build sandcastles, splash in the waves, and enjoy the sun.

Day 2: Maui Ocean Center and Snorkeling Adventure
- Begin your day by visiting the Maui Ocean Center, a world-class aquarium showcasing the marine life found in the surrounding waters.

Discover fascinating exhibits, watch live shows, and let the kids interact with marine creatures through interactive experiences.

- In the afternoon, embark on a snorkeling adventure. Take a family-friendly snorkeling tour to Molokini Crater or explore the coral reefs near Honolua Bay. Snorkeling equipment can be rented or purchased at various rental shops on the island.

Day 3: Maui Tropical Plantation and Iao Valley State Park

- Start the day at the Maui Tropical Plantation, where the whole family can learn about the island's diverse plant life through guided tours and interactive exhibits. Enjoy a tram tour, take a leisurely walk through the plantation, and indulge in tropical treats at the plantation's restaurant.

- In the afternoon, head to Iao Valley State Park, known for its lush greenery and the iconic Iao Needle. Take a family hike along the well-maintained trails, learn about the park's cultural significance, and enjoy breathtaking views of the valley.

Day 4: Adventure at Maui's Upcountry

- Spend the day exploring Maui's Upcountry region. Start by visiting the Ali'i Kula Lavender Farm, where the whole family can wander through vibrant lavender fields, learn about the farm's sustainable practices, and enjoy stunning panoramic views.

- Next, make your way to the Surfing Goat Dairy, where kids can interact with friendly goats and learn about the cheese-making process. Enjoy a delicious goat cheese tasting and perhaps even try your hand at goat milking.

- Wrap up the day with a visit to the Maui Wine tasting room, where adults can sample locally produced wines while kids enjoy refreshing grape juices.

Day 5: Beach Activities and Luau Experience

- Spend the morning enjoying beach activities with the family. Consider booking a surf lesson or renting boogie boards to ride the waves together.

- In the evening, attend a family-friendly luau. Experience traditional Hawaiian music, dance, and feast on a delicious buffet of local cuisine. Enjoy the vibrant performances and immerse yourselves in Hawaiian culture.

Day 6: Adventure at Haleakala National Park

- Rise early for a memorable sunrise experience at Haleakala National Park. Bundle up, as temperatures at the summit can be chilly. Witness the stunning colors as the sun rises above the clouds, creating a breathtaking vista.

- Afterward, explore the park further by taking a family hike along the trails, observing unique flora and fauna, and learning about the volcanic history of Maui.

Day 7: Departure
- Spend your last day in Maui reflecting on your family's incredible experiences. Enjoy a leisurely morning, visit a local bakery for breakfast treats, and take a final stroll along the beach before heading to the airport for your departure.

This family-friendly itinerary offers a mix of beach relaxation, educational experiences, and outdoor adventures, ensuring that every member of the family creates lasting memories of their Maui adventure. Customize the activities based on your family's preferences and interests to make the most of your time on this beautiful island.

Adventure Seekers Itinerary

For adventure seekers looking to experience the thrill of Maui's natural wonders, this itinerary is designed to satisfy your adrenaline cravings. From ziplining through lush forests to hiking to breathtaking waterfalls and exploring vibrant reefs while snorkeling, get ready for an action-packed adventure on the island.

Day 1: Arrival and Beach Time
- Upon arrival, settle into your accommodation and take some time to relax at one of Maui's beautiful beaches. Enjoy the warm sun, swim in the crystal-clear waters, and get energized for the adventures ahead.

Day 2: Ziplining and ATV Excursion
- Start your adventure with an exhilarating ziplining experience. Head to one of Maui's zipline courses, such as the Skyline Eco-Adventures or the Piiholo Ranch Zipline. Soar through the treetops, taking in panoramic views of the island's stunning landscapes.
- In the afternoon, continue the adrenaline rush with an ATV excursion. Navigate through rugged terrains, traversing trails and exploring off-road paths, immersing yourself in Maui's natural beauty.

Day 3: Road to Hana
- Embark on the famous Road to Hana, a scenic drive known for its breathtaking views, waterfalls, and lush rainforests. Rent a car and make stops at must-see attractions like Twin Falls, Wailua Valley State Wayside, and the black sand beach at Waianapanapa State Park. Take short hikes to

hidden waterfalls, swim in natural pools, and capture stunning photos along the way.

Day 4: Snorkeling and Scuba Diving
- Dive into the vibrant underwater world of Maui with a snorkeling or scuba diving adventure. Explore Molokini Crater, a volcanic caldera teeming with marine life and crystal-clear waters, or head to Honolua Bay for excellent snorkeling amidst coral reefs and tropical fish. Immerse yourself in the colorful and diverse marine ecosystem that surrounds the island.

Day 5: Haleakala National Park and Mountain Biking
- Rise early to witness a stunning sunrise at Haleakala National Park. After the sunrise experience, embark on a mountain biking adventure down the slopes of Haleakala. Descend through switchbacks and scenic trails, enjoying the thrill of downhill biking while soaking in breathtaking views of the surrounding landscape.

Day 6: Hiking and Waterfall Exploration
- Spend the day exploring Maui's captivating waterfalls and embarking on challenging hikes. Head to the famous Seven Sacred Pools in Ohe'o Gulch and hike along the Pipiwai Trail, which takes you through a bamboo forest and leads to the

majestic Waimoku Falls. Be prepared for a moderate to strenuous hike and bask in the beauty of these cascading waterfalls.

Day 7: Departure
- Take a moment to reflect on your thrilling adventure-filled week on Maui. Spend your last day relaxing at the beach, enjoying water activities, or exploring local shops and restaurants. Say aloha to the island and depart with unforgettable memories.

This adventure seekers' itinerary promises an adrenaline-fueled journey through Maui's natural wonders. Customize the activities based on your preferences and fitness level to ensure an unforgettable and action-packed experience. Get ready to push your limits, explore breathtaking landscapes, and embrace the adventurous spirit of Maui.

Relaxation and Wellness Itinerary

For travelers seeking a peaceful and rejuvenating experience, this itinerary is dedicated to promoting relaxation and wellness. Immerse yourself in Maui's serene atmosphere, indulge in spa treatments, practice yoga on the beach, take leisurely walks along scenic trails, and savor farm-to-table cuisine.

Prioritize self-care and embrace the island's tranquil side.

Day 1: Arrival and Beach Meditation

- Upon arrival, settle into your accommodation and take a moment to unwind. Head to the beach and find a quiet spot to practice meditation. Let the sound of the ocean waves and the gentle breeze guide you into a state of relaxation and presence.

Day 2: Spa Day and Sunset Yoga

- Treat yourself to a day of pampering and relaxation at one of Maui's renowned spas. Indulge in a massage, rejuvenating facial, or body treatment to ease any tensions and restore your well-being.
- In the evening, join a sunset yoga session on the beach. Let the soothing sounds of the ocean accompany your yoga practice, connecting your mind, body, and spirit as you bask in the golden hues of the sunset.

Day 3: Scenic Coastal Walk and Farm-to-Table Dining

- Begin the day with a leisurely walk along Maui's scenic coastal trails. The Kapalua Coastal Trail or the Wailea Beach Path offer breathtaking ocean views and a serene atmosphere. Take your time to connect with nature and find moments of tranquility along the way.
- In the evening, indulge in a farm-to-table dining experience. Maui's culinary scene emphasizes fresh, locally sourced ingredients. Choose a restaurant that embraces sustainable practices and enjoy a delicious meal that nourishes both your body and soul.

Day 4: Hana Labyrinth and Waterfall Pools
- Visit the Hana Labyrinth, a peaceful and sacred space for contemplation and mindfulness. Take a meditative walk through the labyrinth, allowing your mind to quiet and your spirit to find solace in the serene surroundings.
- Afterward, continue your journey to the enchanting waterfalls along the Road to Hana. Take a refreshing dip in the natural pools of Ohe'o Gulch or explore lesser-known waterfalls, such as the Wailua Falls. Let the cascading water and lush surroundings instill a sense of peace within you.

Day 5: Stand-Up Paddleboarding and Beach Picnic
- Engage in a relaxing water activity by trying stand-up paddleboarding. Glide across the calm waters, connecting with the rhythm of the ocean. Enjoy the tranquility and the stunning coastal views as you paddle along.
- Have a beach picnic and savor a delicious spread of fresh fruits, organic snacks, and refreshing beverages. Take your time to savor each bite, appreciating the flavors and the beauty of the surroundings.

Day 6: Gardens and Botanical Treasures
- Explore Maui's enchanting gardens and botanical treasures. Visit the Ali'i Kula Lavender Farm, where the soothing scent of lavender fills the air, and take a leisurely walk through the vibrant gardens.
- Continue your journey to the Maui Nui Botanical Gardens, which showcase native Hawaiian plants and their cultural significance. Stroll through the serene

pathways, surrounded by beautiful flora, and take a moment to connect with nature.

Day 7: Departure
- Spend your last day in Maui reflecting on your peaceful and rejuvenating journey. Take a morning yoga class or enjoy a leisurely stroll along the beach. Breathe in the island's tranquility and carry the sense of calm with you as you depart.

This relaxation and wellness itinerary encourages you to embrace Maui's serene atmosphere and prioritize self-care. Customize the activities based on your preferences and indulge in experiences that help you unwind, rejuvenate, and foster a deep sense of tranquility. Allow the island's natural beauty to nurture your well-being and create a truly rejuvenating experience.

CONCLUSION

As your journey through the pages of this Maui travel guide comes to a close, we hope that you have found inspiration, practical information, and a sense of excitement for your upcoming visit to the beautiful island of Maui. Embracing the Aloha spirit, you will embark on a remarkable adventure filled with natural wonders, cultural immersion, thrilling activities, and moments of relaxation and rejuvenation.

Maui, with its diverse landscapes, vibrant culture, and warm hospitality, offers an unparalleled experience that will leave you with memories to last a lifetime. From the stunning beaches of Kaanapali and Wailea to the lush rainforests of Hana and the majestic Haleakala National Park, each corner of Maui unveils a new facet of its captivating charm.

Immerse yourself in the island's rich history and cultural significance, explore the vibrant towns, indulge in the tantalizing flavors of Hawaiian cuisine, and discover the wonders of Maui's underwater world. Engage in thrilling adventures such as surfing, hiking to waterfalls, and zip-lining, or simply unwind and find solace in the tranquil beauty of the island.

Throughout your journey, embrace the Aloha spirit, a guiding principle of love, compassion, and respect. Interact with the locals, learn about their traditions, and immerse yourself in the spirit of Aloha, which will undoubtedly enhance your experience and foster a deeper connection with the island.

As you explore Maui's regions, seek out the best beaches, indulge in the local cuisine, and immerse yourself in cultural immersion, always remember to respect the environment, follow safety guidelines, and be mindful of the island's delicate ecosystems.

With insider tips, practical information, this guide equips you with the tools to navigate Maui with ease, ensuring that your adventure unfolds seamlessly. Whether you are traveling with family, seeking thrilling adventures, or simply looking to relax and rejuvenate, Maui offers a wealth of experiences that cater to every traveler's desires.

So, as you embark on your Maui journey, let the spirit of Aloha guide you, let the natural wonders inspire you, and let the warmth of the island's hospitality envelop you. Create cherished memories, connect with the beauty of Maui's landscapes, and take a piece of the island's enchantment home with you.

May your time in Maui be filled with joy, discovery, and a sense of wonder. Embrace the Aloha spirit and allow Maui to leave an indelible mark on your heart, ensuring that your memories of this island paradise will last a lifetime.

Happy Travel

Thank You for Reading!

I would like to express my heartfelt gratitude for joining me on this journey through the enchanting island of Maui. I hope that this travel guide has provided you with valuable insights, inspiration, and practical information to make your visit to Maui truly unforgettable.

Remember to embrace the Aloha spirit, immerse yourself in the beauty of the island, and create memories that will last a lifetime. Whether you find yourself lounging on pristine beaches, exploring the lush rainforests, indulging in local cuisine, or engaging in thrilling adventures, may your time in Maui be filled with joy, wonder, and a deep connection with this tropical paradise.

As you embark on your Maui adventure, I extend my warmest wishes for a safe and fulfilling journey. Thank you for choosing to explore the wonders of Maui with me, and we hope that this guide has been a valuable companion throughout your exploration of the island.

Wishing you an extraordinary experience as you discover the magic of Maui and create treasured memories that will stay with you long after your visit. Mahalo nui loa (Thank you very much) for reading, and may your time in Maui be filled with Aloha!

With warmest regards,
Willie F. Smith

Made in the USA
Middletown, DE
29 October 2023

41575809R00066